(OULD YOU EVER?

Speak Chimpanzee

By Dr. David Darling

DILLON PRESS, INC.
Minneapolis, Minnesota 55415

Library of Congress Cataloging-in-Publication Data

Darling, David J.
  Could you ever speak chimpanzee? /
  David Darling.
      p.   cm.

  Summary: Explores how animals communicate and whether people will ever be
able to communicate with them.
    ISBN 0-87518-448-0 : $14.95
    1. Animal communication—Juvenile litera-
ture.   2. Human—animal communication—
Juvenile literature.   [1. Animal communication.   2. Human-animal communication.]
I. Title.
QL776.D37   1990
591.59—dc20   90-35040
                                        CIP
                                         AC

Dillon Press, Inc., 242 Portland Avenue South
Minneapolis, Minnesota 55415

Printed in the United States of America
1 2 3 4 5 6 7 8 9 10 99 98 97 96 95 94 93 92 91 90

Photographic Acknowledgments

The photographs are reproduced through
the courtesy of Scott Camazine; John Can-
calosi; Densey Clyne, Mantis Wildlife
Films/Oxford Scientific Films; Christopher
Crowley; Gerry Ellis and Michael Osmond/
Ellis Wildlife Collection; Beatrix and Robert Gardner, Department of Psychology,
University of Nevada-Reno; George H. Har-
rison, from Grant Heilman; Photo Researchers, Inc./Toni Angermayer, Tom
McHugh; Gail Shumway; Elizabeth Rubert,
Language Research Center; and Amy Ved-
der/Bill Weber.

METRIC CONVERSION CHART To Find Approximate Equivalents		
WHEN YOU KNOW:	**MULTIPLY BY:**	**TO FIND:**
TEMPERATURE degrees Fahrenheit (minus 32)	0.56	degrees Celsius
LENGTH		
feet	30.48	centimeters
yards	0.91	meters
miles	1.61	kilometers
MASS (weight)		
pounds	0.45	kilograms
tons	0.91	metric tons
VOLUME		
cubic yards	0.77	cubic meters
AREA		
acres	0.41	hectares
square miles	2.59	square kilometers
CAPACITY		
gallons	3.79	liters

Contents

The Challenge

Now listen, Doctor, and I'll tell you something. Did you know that animals can talk?"

"I know that parrots can talk," said the Doctor.

"Oh, we parrots can talk in two **languages***—people's language and bird language," said Polynesia proudly.

With these words, Polynesia the parrot began the first lesson in animal speech to her famous owner, Doctor Dolittle.

Unfortunately, the Doctor Dolittle stories by Hugh Lofting are only make-believe. Yet, it is a fact that animals of the same type, or **species**, do **communicate** among themselves. For example, they can warn each other of approaching danger or pass news about the location of food. Animals of different species can swap information, too. A lioness that snarls at a pack of hyenas trying to steal her kill is sending a clear message to the intruders: "Back off, or else!"

Animals such as this "smiling" mandrill communicate in different ways. The mandrill is a large baboon that lives in western Africa.

Every day, we humans also communicate with other animals. When I call out to my dog, "Come here" or "Stay" or "Sit," he usually obeys. In return, he sends signals to me. By wagging his tail or letting it droop between his legs, by barking or whimpering, and in many other ways, he lets me know how he feels.

Some animals are much easier for us to communicate with than others. A dog or horse can

*Words in **bold type** are explained in the glossary at the end of this book.

learn to respond to a wide variety of spoken commands. But try training a slug or a beetle to come when you call it!

How well we can communicate with another animal depends mainly on that creature's intelligence. The cleverest of species, such as gorillas, chimpanzees, dolphins, and whales, are usually the ones with the most complicated language of their own. They are also the species with which we may communicate most effectively in the future.

So, could you ever speak chimpanzee (or gorilla or dolphin)? Although "talking with the animals" may never be quite as simple as Doctor Dolittle found it, a great deal of interesting progress has already been made. But before we consider possible communication between humans and other species, it will be helpful to look at some of the strange and varied forms of language in the animal kingdom.

▌A luna moth.

Two long-eared baby owls puff up their feathers to make themselves look larger and fiercer. In this way, they try to discourage an attack by a predator.

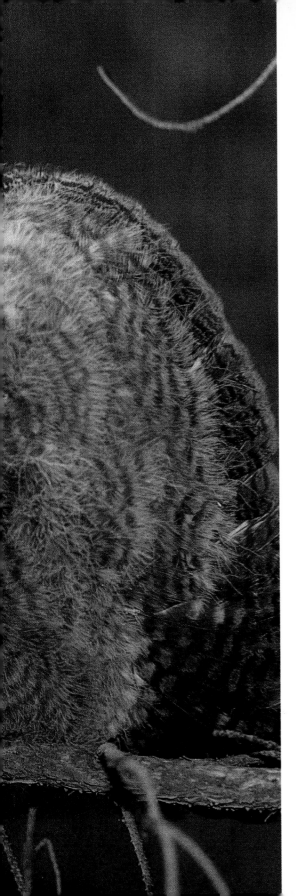

Animal Chatter

Birds sing, wolves howl, dolphins click— nearly every animal on earth communicates in some way with others of its kind. Animals have reasons for sending messages. At certain times an individual needs to attract a mate. At other times it has to defend its territory against competing creatures. Some species, such as ants, depend for their very lives on working closely together as a team. To do this, they must constantly exchange messages.

Many animals rely heavily on communication by sound, just as humans do. Finches, for instance, use as many as 25 different calls to inform each other of the presence of food or enemies. They even have special warning calls to let other finches know if an attacker is in the air or on the ground.

Sound, though, is not the only way to pass on information in the animal world. Smell, taste, touch, and body movement can be just as important.

Jive in the Hive

Honeybees have one of the strangest ways to tell each other the location of a new food supply. When a worker bee has found some flowers containing nectar, it flies back to its hive and starts to dance on the surface of the honeycomb.

If the nectar is fairly close to the hive, the returning bee performs what is called a round dance. It turns in small circles, first to the left and then to the right. Other workers, by crowding around and constantly touching the dancing bee, learn that the food source is nearby. From the speed and length of the dance, they also find out whether the supply of nectar is rich or poor.

If the nectar is more than about 100 yards away, the messenger bee performs a more complicated routine known as a waggle dance. This time, the bee

8

first does a short, straight run, waggling its body as it goes. Then it veers off to one side and returns in a half-circle to its starting point. After the next straight, waggling run, it goes back in a half-circle on the other side, making a kind of figure-eight pattern. The direction of the straight run tells the other bees exactly which way they must fly to locate the food. The faster the waggle dance is performed, the shorter the distance to the nectar.

The honeybees have an amazing system—a simple language based on body movement, as well as smell and sound. But it is hard to believe that creatures so small actually think about what they are doing. Their language is almost certainly one of pure

Numbered honeybees in a hive. Honeybees use body movement, smell, and sound to send messages to other bees in the hive.

instinct. In other words, they are born able to communicate in this way; they do not have to learn it.

In 1988, scientists at University College, Cardiff, in Wales, reported the most detailed study yet of bees' brains. The researchers sliced up each tiny brain into extremely thin sections. Then, by staining the slices with various colored dyes, they were able to identify each part of the brain and build a kind of atlas of the brain's structure. This atlas will now be used in further work to discover what parts of a bee's brain control tasks such as decision-making and communication.

Ant Attack!

Alone, an army ant will quickly die. But as part of an enormous swarm, it is one of the most successful—and deadly—creatures in the world. Nothing can survive in the path of army ants when they are raiding for food.

Like bees, ants are **social** insects. That means they always live together in large groups. Each insect works not for itself, but for the good of the whole colony.

Also like bees, ants communicate in an unusual

way. Chemicals produced by the queen ant are picked up by the workers that attend to her needs. These chemicals tell the workers what task has to be carried out next. At great speed, the chemical message is spread throughout the colony by the ants rubbing antennas with one another.

In the case of army ants, the queen's changing body chemicals cause quite dramatic effects in the swarm's behavior. At a signal from the queen, hundreds of thousands of ants march across the forest

Green tree ants, also known as Australian weaver ants, join leaves together to make a nest.

floor like a brown river, attacking any creatures in their path. A different signal from the queen instructs the colony to make camp for the night. The workers hook their legs together to form a living **bivouac**, or temporary camp, in a hollow tree or other sheltered place. The queen and her young are

protected deep inside.

Insects such as ants and bees seem to act intelligently when they behave in this way. It is as if the queen ant, for instance, knew what needed to be done next and then sent out the appropriate signal. But, in fact, all insects act upon instinct. Not even the well-organized army ants really think about what they are doing or plan ahead. The way they behave is programmed into them from birth, just as a computer is programmed to carry out certain tasks over and over again.

Since insects do communicate, we can say that they have a very simple language. But that language is very fixed. It has not changed over millions of years, nor will it change in the future. Ants and bees and creatures like them cannot learn new ideas.

Although we may discover how they communicate among themselves, they could never understand any messages from us.

If we are to have meaningful two-way communication with other species, it will not be with creatures as simple as insects. Instead, we must look at larger, brainier species and at the way they communicate.

An Incredible Sense of Smell

Of all the signals that pass back and forth between animals, the most important are those that bring male and female together for mating and breeding. Without this kind of communication, a species would rapidly die out.

One of the most incredible signaling systems for attracting mates is that of the **Luna moth**. The antennas of the male Luna moth are so sensitive that it can detect the scent of a female, in the dark, from a distance of seven miles!

Saying It Without Words

How do you tell someone else that you are frightened, worried, happy, or angry if you cannot use human words? Animals have developed an incredible variety of signaling systems to get their point across.

A cat threatened by a strange dog will suddenly hiss, raise its tail, and arch its back. This is like saying, "I'm frightened, but if you come any closer, I'll attack." If you have seen this happen, you will have

little doubt that the dog understands the message! At the very least, the dog will back off, and often it loses interest in the cat.

Cats, dogs, and many other types of animals are highly **territorial**. In other words, they regard a certain patch of ground as their own and will fight to defend it. Dogs mark the boundaries of their territory with urine. Deer, on the other hand, give off a strong-smelling substance called musk from the corners of their eyes. They rub the musk onto trees at the edge of their territory. Other animals recognize these scent warnings and usually stay away from those areas.

The most important signals are the ones that

affect an animal's chance of survival. Most species do not engage in idle chatter. Instead, they have a limited **vocabulary** of sounds and movements, which they use only when necessary. The more complicated the creature's life-style, the more involved its language tends to be.

Black-headed gulls—seabirds that nest in large, crowded colonies—can send at least 30 different messages in their language. They can also convey shades of meaning by small changes in their **posture**, or body position, or by the loudness of their calls. Yet their language has only 17 distinct signals. How then can they send so many different messages?

When it sends a message, the black-headed gull often joins several basic signals together to make a new signal. For instance, the gull has three separate ways of posturing to threaten a rival that is coming too near. But if those three signals are displayed together in a certain order, then they take on a completely different meaning. They become a courtship signal—a signal meant to attract a mate.

The gull also extends its range of messages by interpreting signals in different ways at different times. We do this a great deal in our own language. For instance, the sound of the *tea* you drink is exactly like that of the *tee* used for holding up a golf ball. Yet from the way in which the word is used, you can tell what is meant by it. In the same way, the "choking" display of the black-headed gull has different meanings depending on the situation. During courtship, it is used by a male bird to send a message to a passing female: "I own this bit of land, and it would make a good nest!" But later, when the male has won his mate, the same display warns other birds, "I own this bit of land, so stay away!"

Some members of the crow family have an even more complex language. In fact, their babies have to learn crow-talk, just as children must learn a language such as English. Young jackdaws, for instance, often show no fear of an approaching **predator** such as a cat. Only when an adult jackdaw has swooped down, making an urgent rattling call to warn them, do the youngsters recognize the danger. Afterward, the young birds know immediately to connect the rattling call of their elders with a cat or another threat to their safety.

At the University of Rochester in New York, Kathy

and Ernest Nordeen have been studying communication between zebra finches. In 1988, they reported that a male finch spends the first three or four weeks out of its egg just listening to the songs of older birds. Then, for the next month, it practices until its own singing becomes perfect. During this period of learning, the Nordeens discovered, about 18,000 new cells grow in the young finch's brain. Cells are the tiny living units that make up every part of an animal's body. Surprisingly, more than

A baby elephant raises its trunk to signal to its mother that it needs help or wants attention.

Tuning In to Sounds

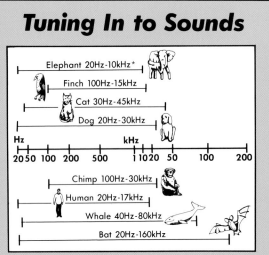

Elephant 20Hz-10kHz*
Finch 100Hz-15kHz
Cat 30Hz-45kHz
Dog 20Hz-30kHz

Hz   kHz
20 50 100 200 500   1 10 20 50   100   200

Chimp 100Hz-30kHz
Human 20Hz-17kHz
Whale 40Hz-80kHz
Bat 20Hz-160kHz

*1,000 Hertz equals 1 kHz

Hearing plays a vital part in animal communication. The range of sounds that can be sensed varies greatly from species to species. Many animal predators need to hear sounds of a higher **pitch** than humans can hear because much of their prey makes high-pitched squeaks. The pitch of sound—its highness or lowness—can be measured in **Hertz** (Hz). This is the number of times a sound wave vibrates in a second. The chart above shows the range over which a number of animals can "tune in" to their surroundings.

half of the new cells in the finch's brain help the bird remember its songs!

Essential Information

To discover how well humans may be able to "talk" with other species, we must know the amount of information that animals can send to one another.

Most of the signaling done in the animal world has to do only with survival. If you are a jackdaw being stalked by the neighborhood cat, all you need is for your friends to yell "cat!" in bird language. It would not help to know the cat's color, or its owner's name, or the exact length of its whiskers, if you were about to be eaten.

Because most animals spend much of their time trying to stay alive, their languages are short, simple, and to the point. The calls they make, their **gestures** and other signals, carry only the most essential information. *A predator is coming! Be my mate! Go away! Feed me! Help me!* Since these are the messages that really matter, they are often the only things for which the creature has a signal.

Yet not all animal languages are quite so simple. And not all animals are so set in their ways that they cannot learn new signals or adapt to new situations.

A green monkey in Barbados, an island in the West Indies, calls out to send a message to other monkeys. Does it know what it is communicating?

The Secret Codes of Monkeys

Animals communicate important messages that can mean the difference between life and death. But do they know what they are communicating? And are the animals that receive the messages aware of what they mean?

Because we are aware of meaning in our speech and writing, it is natural for us to think that other creatures use language in the same way. Yet, in fact, much animal language is instinctive. The signaler often has no idea of the goal of its actions. The receiver, too, may react in a purely automatic, unthinking way.

Conversation between humans and a creature whose language relies entirely on instinct could never get very far. If such a creature responded at all to our signals, it would be in a dull, machinelike way. That would be the same as saying that a pianist has conversations with a piano, because when he or she presses a key, the instrument replies with a note!

But are there any animals that really understand what they are saying or hearing? Can any of them

exchange signals about more than just their basic feelings?

Until quite recently, most experts would have answered "no" to these questions. They would have argued that no animals, except for humans, can express anything more than raw emotion— a cry of warning, for instance, or a scream of rage. Those experts would have claimed that no animal could invent or understand labels for things in the way that we do.

But now that view has changed. New studies have shown that some species do have a language in which labels and codes play an important part.

Clues Out of Africa
During the late 1960s, researcher Tom Struhsaker of

Eagle Alarm

Leopard Alarm

Snake Alarm

the New York Zoological Society carried out a study of **vervet monkeys** in Kenya's Amboseli National Park. He discovered that vervets have different alarm calls for their three main enemies: leopards, eagles, and snakes. Most interesting of all, he found that each type of call caused the vervets that heard it to behave in a very different way—a way that would help protect them from that particular predator.

When the vervets heard a "leopard" alarm call, they would scamper up the nearest trees. An "eagle"

Vervet monkeys respond in different ways to alarm calls for their three main predators: leopards, eagles, and snakes.

call caused the monkeys to look up at the sky and head for thick, low-lying bushes. Finally, a "snake" call made the animals up stand on their hind legs and peer into the long grass around them.

These findings by Struhsaker led to a lot of debate among scientists. Most experts at the time did not believe that the vervets actually understood what each of their alarm calls meant. According to this view, the monkey giving the alarm call simply cried out most excitedly if it saw a leopard, less strongly for an eagle, and least of all for a snake. Reacting to how excited the caller sounded, the other monkeys looked around and saw for themselves what kind of predator was coming. Then they responded to the danger in the most appropriate way.

A few scientists, though, had a different explanation. They claimed that the vervets' alarm calls stood for the ideas of *leopard, eagle,* and *snake.* In other words, the vervets used a language in which certain ideas or objects were represented by certain sounds. That is exactly what humans do in languages all the time. But the notion that another species might also use labels for objects and ideas was quite bold and new.

24

❙ A vervet monkey with baby in Kenya, East Africa.

■ Alex the parrot with Dr. Irene Pepperberg.

The Conversational Parrot

For more than 10 years, Irene Pepperberg of Northwestern University in Evanston, Illinois, has been training an African gray parrot named Alex. He now speaks the correct English words for 30 different objects, six colors, five shapes, and quantities from one to six. Unlike other talking birds, Alex uses these words in the right way at the right time. He learned the word *gray*, for instance, by asking the color of his reflection in the mirror. He will ask for objects that he wants and will even ask for "tickling." Alex has shown that real conversations are possible between humans and animals, and that he, at least, is no bird-brain!

In the years that followed, further studies confirmed that vervets really do use a labeling system. What is more, other kinds of monkeys appear to understand language in the same way. Toque **macaques** in Sri Lanka, for instance, have special calls that an individual will use if it comes across an especially large supply of food or a favorite food plant. Other macaques become excited when they hear such a call, even when the food is out of sight. This behavior suggests that they understand exactly what the call means.

Following the pioneering efforts by Struhsaker and others, more and more researchers began to observe how monkeys and their relatives communicate. Soon this was to lead to another remarkable discovery.

26

Hidden Signals

For years, scientists had assumed that all animals communicate only by instinct or by displays of basic emotion. Now, the scientists knew that some creatures could use simple "words" to describe objects that were familiar and important to them. If these animals could use language in this way, then they might be able to learn new words or labels from a human teacher.

Still, the ability of the vervets and other monkeys to communicate appeared to be limited. Although they used a language based on words or labels, their vocabulary seemed to be quite small. They could signal to each other with a few different grunts and

Scientists have studied the way monkeys such as macaques use language. These lion-tailed macaques live in Southeast Asia.

27

chatters. That was all they could say—or was it?

If you listen to people speaking quickly in a foreign language, much of what they say appears to be run together. It is hard to tell where one word ends and another begins, because you have no idea what the sounds mean. Your ear has not been trained to pick out the small, separate sounds of the language. Could it be that we make the same mistake when listening to the "speech" of other animals?

To find out, Steven Green of the University of Florida made various recordings of the "coo" call of Japanese macaques. Each recording was made in a different situation. He then passed these recordings through a special instrument that spread apart the sound and displayed exactly what it looked like on a chart. To the human ear, all coos of Japanese macaques sound the same. Green's results, though, showed just how easily we can be fooled. Each coo, when plotted out, followed a different pattern. It became clear that the macaques were using not just one call over and over again, but a wide variety of different calls depending on the situation.

Certain grunts that vervet monkeys make when they meet each other also sound identical to our ears. But again, when examined closely, these grunts turn out to be quite different. As far as the vervets are concerned, they have completely different meanings. Studies of other monkeys have shown the same secret inner structure to their language.

Perhaps it is not surprising that monkey language should be similar in some ways to our own, even if it is much simpler. Physically, humans and monkeys share many characteristics. But there is one group of animals to which we are even more closely related. That group, which includes the chimpanzee and the gorilla, is the **apes**.

Young gorillas play while an adult watches. Apes are known for their ability to communicate.

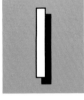

Ape Talk

In zoos around the world, one of the most popular attractions is the apes. Chimpanzees, gorillas, orangutans, and gibbons—the four main types of apes—remind us so much of ourselves that we find them fascinating. Of all living species, they are the ones we are most closely related to, both in behavior and form.

Like us, apes have nimble fingers that can delicately hold and grasp things. Often, apes stand and walk upright. They look after their young with as much care as a human parent. And, like humans, they have large brains and expressive faces.

In the wild, apes are inventive

users of tools. Chimpanzees, for example, will often dip a stem of grass into a termite mound to attract the insects inside it, a favorite food. Chimpanzees will also squeeze a leaf "sponge" to get water out of a tight crack. Raised in captivity, apes show off their creative and problem-solving powers in other ways. Chimpanzees will paint lively, colorful paintings like those of a young child, while orangutans are well known to zookeepers as clever escape artists. In some ways, then, apes seem to think and act as humans do.

Apes are great communicators among themselves, too. Researchers such as Dian Fossey (mountain gorillas), Jane Goodall (chimpanzees), and George Schaller have watched and recorded dozens of ways in which these creatures exchange messages. Schaller noticed that, when startled, a gorilla would stand still and shake its head back and forth. Taking this to mean, "It's all right, I intend no harm," Schaller then started making this sign himself whenever he came across a gorilla unexpectedly in the forest. In a simple way, the scientist was communicating with the creature in its own language.

Although apes use a wide range of sounds and

facial expressions to communicate with one another, their language seems to be quite basic. They appear to "talk" only about things and events that affect their immediate situation. Like dogs, cats, and other animals, apes send messages about their most important feelings and needs at that moment. Their own language does not seem to deal with ideas that are connected with the past or future.

It is possible that an ape's brain cannot handle more complicated thoughts. On the other hand, the

A chimpanzee uses a leaf as a sponge for drinking.

animals may simply lack the necessary communication skills. This is a vital point. For if apes can think about complex ideas, we may be able to teach them enough of our own language for them to be able to carry on a conversation with us.

Signs of Hope

Starting about 50 years ago, several attempts were made to train apes to speak English. Usually, this involved taking a newborn chimpanzee into a household with a newborn baby, and raising both together in the same way. The two youngsters had twin cribs, twin high chairs, and even diaper pails! At the end of three years, the young chimp was far ahead of the human infant in its ability to climb, run, and jump. But while the child had already mastered several hundred spoken words, the chimp could only make, with great difficulty, simple sounds such as *Mama, Papa,* and *cup.*

At the time, experiments such as these appeared to show that chimps, and other apes, could not reason or think about language in the way humans do. But later, two scientists from the University of Nevada, Beatrix and Robert Gardner, offered a different explanation for the chimps' failure to learn spoken English. Chimps, gorillas, and other apes, they pointed out, are not physically equipped to make humanlike sounds. They cannot speak like humans because their mouths and vocal chords do not work in the same way. Also, these animals use their voices only when excited.

To find out if apes could learn to communicate in English, the Gardners realized that a completely new approach had to be tried. In fact, there was one way of carrying on a conversation, without speech, that already existed. This method was used by people who had difficulty hearing or talking. It was the American sign language, or Ameslan.

Over the next few years, a number of chimps were given lessons in how to use Ameslan. The language lessons have produced some exciting results. Not only have these animals learned how to sign as many as 200 English words, but they even created new words and phrases.

For instance, on seeing a pair of swans in a pond, a young female chimp called Washoe made the signs for *water* and *bird* together. In this way, Washoe invented her own label for a swan—*waterbird*. On another occasion, after she had noticed a small doll lying in her cup of water, Washoe signed *Baby in my drink!* No one had taught Washoe how to put these words together in that particular order before. It was clear that the young chimp knew how to use sign language in an intelligent and meaningful way.

Once, a reporter for the *New York Times*, Bryce Rensberger, went to visit Washoe in order to write a story about her. Both of Rensberger's parents could neither speak nor hear. Although Rensberger himself had normal hearing, he had to learn Ameslan as a child to be able to communicate with his mother

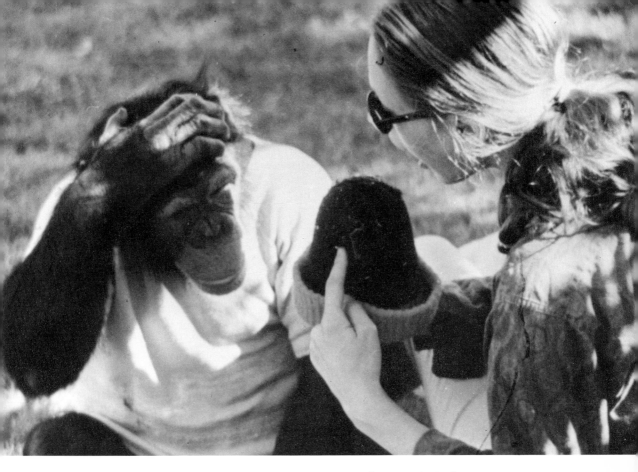

Using American
Sign Language,
Washoe makes the
sign for *hat*.

and father. Indeed, he regarded Ameslan as his first language. After spending some time with Washoe, Rensberger made a remarkable discovery. "Suddenly," he reported, "I realized I was conversing with a member of another species in my native tongue."

Conversations With Kanzi

Encouraged by the success of Washoe and other chimps in learning Ameslan, other researchers have tried to teach apes different forms of sign language. At the Language Research Center in Atlanta, Georgia, scientists have developed a new language called Yerkish. To communicate in Yerkish, an ape presses keys on a special computer keyboard that is marked with various signs, or **symbols**. The computer records everything the ape "says," even during the night when no humans are present.

By tapping the keys in just the right order, the ape can ask the computer for water, juice, candy, and even music or movies. In this way, researchers found that one chimpanzee, Lana, seemed to prefer jazz music to rock music and movies about chimps to movies about human beings. But the computer cannot supply every need. One night, perhaps feeling sorry for herself, Lana punched the keys for "Please, machine, tickle Lana!"

The most remarkable results using the computer at the Language Research Center have been obtained with Kanzi, a pygmy chimpanzee. Pygmy chimps are slightly smaller than the common species of chimpanzee. In fact, some specialists consider them to be the most humanlike of all animals. That belief has been supported by Kanzi's language achievements, which have gone beyond those of any other ape tested so far.

"I was astounded when the evidence began to appear that Kanzi was acquiring symbols simul-

Kanzi examines the symbols displayed on a portable keyboard.

taneously with spoken English," said Dr. Sue Savage-Rumbaugh in 1985. By this, the scientists meant that Kanzi was learning more than how to use the computer keyboard. He was also learning the meaning of words and sentences that were spoken to him. If asked, for instance, "Will you go and get a nappy for your sister Mulika?" he would do it.

Kanzi shows, too, an amazing ability to put words together without training. He identifies objects by name and comments on what he is doing. He even describes actions that he intends to carry out in the future. This shows that the pygmy chimp can plan ahead and then communicate what he is going to do. It also shows that, while there may be no way

39

The Future of Apes

Like many other animal species, all of the great apes—gorillas, chimpanzees, and orangutans—are in danger of becoming **extinct** in the wild. They are disappearing because people are still hunting apes, even though this is now banned, and are destroying the forests in which they live. According to a recent estimate, one acre of the world's tropical forests is cut down or burned every second.

Most endangered of all the apes is the mountain gorilla. Thanks largely to the efforts of one woman, Dian Fossey, the gentle nature of this magnificent animal, as well as dangers to its life, have become known to the world.

For many years, Dian Fossey studied mountain gorillas in their last remaining stronghold, the Virunga Mountains of Rwanda, Zaire, and Uganda. She set up the Karisoke Research Centre in Rwanda's Parc National des Volcans. Fossey spent day after day sitting in the forest, watching every movement the gorillas made.

A group of mountain gorillas in the part of Africa where Dian Fossey studied these great apes and worked to save them from extinction.

Eventually, she won the trust of these animals. In fact, they allowed her to live among them and even to groom the great silverback males—the leaders of gorilla packs.

Tragically, Dian Fossey was murdered by poachers in 1986. Since then, the film *Gorillas in the Mist* has told to millions of people worldwide the remarkable story of her life and achievements.

to express such thoughts in the animal's own language, Kanzi's brain is able to learn a new language in which such expression is possible.

Though Kanzi rarely makes up complete sentences with his keyboard, he does create two- or three-word statements, often without prompting. Once, his fellow chimp, Austin, was moved out of the compound for a time. Kanzi seemed to miss his usual bedtime visit with his friend. But he quickly solved the problem. After several lonely nights,

Kanzi typed the symbols for *Austin* and *TV* on his keyboard. When a videotape of Austin was played, Kanzi settled happily into his nest for the night!

Language and Brains

Language research seems to show that apes do not have a more advanced language of their own because they cannot make the range of sounds that humans can. But if they are taught sign language, they are capable of using words and ideas in a much more complicated way than they do in the wild.

Not all scientists, however, would agree with this. A few researchers maintain that chimps and other apes simply copy what humans do when they use Ameslan. This is the same, they say, as a parrot that mimics what is said to it without understanding what the words mean. Most scientists, though, believe that the achievements of apes such as Washoe and Kanzi are based on real language ability, not mimicry.

One big difference between apes and most other animals is their relatively large brain. The heavier a creature's brain is compared with the weight of the rest of its body, the more intelligent it is likely to be.

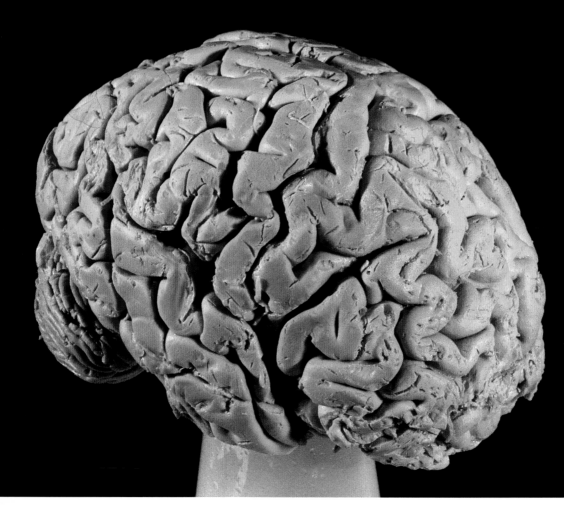

The higher an animal's intelligence, the greater its language skills are likely to be.

Humans have a heavy brain for the weight of their bodies. Even more important, much of the human brain consists of a region called the **cortex**. In this part of the brain, all types of higher thinking, such as imagination, understanding, and reasoning, are carried out. Parts of the cortex are also responsible for our speech and language abilities.

The brain of a chimpanzee is similar to that of a

human being. The chimp's brain, too, has a relatively large cortex, although it is only about one-third the size of a person's. The difference in size may explain why a chimp cannot make up or understand long sentences or complex ideas.

It seems, however, that chimps are unexpectedly good at basic math problems. In 1987, Dr. Sue Savage-Rumbaugh and two colleagues announced that the chimps they had been studying could quickly pick out which of two pairs of dishes on separate trays contained the most chocolates. Chimps may, the scientists concluded, have an ability similar to that of humans to estimate how many objects there are in a group.

Other species of animals also have unusually big brains with large cortexes. In fact, some of these creatures have brains that are bigger than a chimp's in relation to the size of their bodies. Yet far less is known about them, and their behavior and language, than any ape. These fascinating, intelligent creatures do not live on land where they can easily be studied, but in the world's vast oceans.

A humpback whale breaches, or leaps above, the ocean's surface.

Songsters of the Sea

More than two-thirds of the planet's surface is covered by ocean, most of it unexplored. This is the home of the **cetaceans**, a remarkable group of animals that includes whales, dolphins, and porpoises.

Cetaceans swim and feed in the water like fish. They have the same sleek shapes and fins as fish. But, like humans, they are warm-blooded, air-breathing mammals. The females do not lay eggs, but give birth to live babies which they feed with milk.

Among the cetaceans are the largest animals ever to have lived on earth. Biggest of all is the blue whale, a creature so huge that it may weigh as much as 32 elephants and be as long as three school buses. In a day, a blue whale can eat 9,000 pounds of food, and in a single swallow it can gulp down 100 pounds!

One of the most surprising features of cetaceans, though, is the size of their brains. At 20 pounds, the brain of the sperm whale is the heaviest of any animal—six times the weight of the heaviest human brain. Even the familiar bottlenose dolphin, often seen performing at places such as Sea World, has a slightly bigger brain than that of an adult man or woman.

Whale Thoughts

Though some whales have very large brains, this does not mean they are smarter than human beings. As with the apes, brain size alone is not an accurate guide to intelligence. What matters more is brain size in relation to body size. Measured in this way, whales are less intelligent than humans because they weigh hundreds of times as much. Much of their brain, according to some scientists, is needed just to control their huge bodies.

Yet, it may not be as simple as that. When scientists examined the brains of whales in detail, they

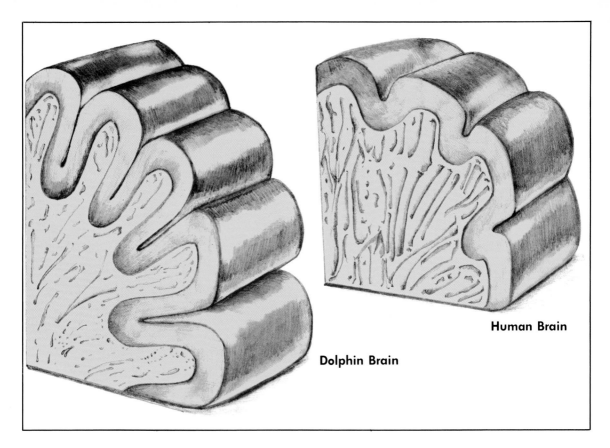

Human Brain

Dolphin Brain

found that the brains are especially well developed in those areas normally devoted to higher thought. Whales have unusually large cortexes.

Researchers know that in humans, the front part of the brain is important in the ability to make decisions, to solve problems, and to think about the future or the past. Scientists also believe that the amount of folding on the front part of the brain is related to intelligence. Human brains, for instance, are more folded than chimpanzee brains. These, in turn, are more folded than rabbit brains.

The front part of many whale brains is very large, very folded, and contains a much greater number of brain cells than a human brain does. It

Dolphins have twice as many folds as people do in the front part of the brain.

seems unlikely that this region of a whale's brain would have anything to do with controlling the animal's great body. Instead, it is probably used for advanced thinking, just as it is in humans. Still, we do not know for sure.

Whales are difficult to study because they live so differently than humans. They live in the water, while we live on land. Since whales have fins rather than hands, they cannot make or use tools. We have hands with which we can build homes and machines and change the world around us. Whales leave no trace of their activities on their surroundings. To learn more about whale intelligence, we must look at the way they behave and, most importantly, at the way they communicate.

The Mysterious Giants
Millions of people have watched the playful antics and amazing acrobatics of cetaceans in captivity. Dolphins and killer whales are famous for the tricks they can learn and perform. Yet, that ability alone does not prove that these creatures are especially intelligent. Properly trained, dogs, horses, and even parrots will perform crowd-pleasing stunts on command.

To discover how clever cetaceans really are, they must be studied in the ocean in their natural habitat. After all, human beings may seem much less creative if imprisoned than if they are free to do as they like.

A killer whale performs at Sea World in San Diego, California.

To humans, much of whale behavior remains a mystery. But at least some of the things that whales have been observed doing in the wild suggests they are remarkably good thinkers.

Perhaps the most fascinating evidence that whales may be highly intelligent comes from the

49

sounds they make to each other under the sea. Strange, puzzling, and very complicated, these sounds may be part of a language that we are still far from being able to understand.

The Songs of the Humpback Whale

In the mid-1960s, three scientists from Princeton University, Roger and Katherine Payne and Scott McVay, began a study of the weird moans and cries of humpback whales. First, they listened to tapes that had been made a few years earlier using a hydrophone—an underwater microphone—in the seas around Bermuda. Then, they began making their own hydrophone recordings from a small sailboat. What they

discovered was totally unexpected.

Each year, during the winter months, humpback whales gather in the same part of the ocean to breed. And each year, at this time, the males make their most beautiful sounds, or "songs." At the beginning of each breeding season, all the humpbacks arrive singing the same song. As the season progresses, though, the song gradually changes. By the end of the season, it can hardly be recognized from what it was at the start. All the whales in a given breeding area continue to sing the same song, and all keep up to date with the current version of the song.

During the summer months, when the humpbacks live alone, they do very little singing. But when the breeding season starts again, they gather once more and sing the same song that they ended with the year before. Then the whole cycle is repeated.

Songs from different groups of humpbacks in different parts of the world show little resemblance to one another. The basic rules, however, seem to be followed for changing them. Some scientists believe that whales are born knowing the rules for composing their songs. The whales change the songs according to these rules, and memorize any changes made by nearby singers.

Many animals sing—birds, insects, frogs, bats, and gibbons, to name just a few. But only humpbacks, as far as we know, change their songs from year to year. Why they do this is a complete mystery. The whales may enjoy singing, and their

The Sound World of the Whale

Though whales can see well, that is not much use in detecting objects over long distances under water, even if the water is clear. It is no use at all below depths of 1,200 feet, where the ocean is pitch black. Fortunately, all whales seem to have the ability to find their way in the water and sight their food through **echolocation**.

Not much is known about how whales and dolphins make or hear sounds. It seems that their clicking noises come from air spaces inside the head. Air may be forced back and forth very quickly in these spaces to create the clicks. The sounds then move forward through an oil-filled gap in the creature's forehead. There they are focused into a more power-ful beam, just as a magnifying glass can focus the sun's rays.

When a whale's click strikes a school of fish, it bounces back. What happens next is not certain. The whale may pick up the returning sound with its jawbone. Finally, the sound travels down an oil-filled channel in the jawbone to the inner

Using echolocation, a dolphin identifies a triangle held by a diver *(above)*; a killer whale locates a school of fish a mile away in two seconds *(below)*.

ear. From the time it takes the click to travel out and back again, the whale can judge how far away the fish are.

Experiments with dolphins have shown that their ability to use echolocation is highly developed. For example, a blind-folded dolphin can distinguish triangular shapes from circular ones, or a large cir-cle from a small one. Even more amazing-ly, a dolphin can tell by echolocation alone whether a square object is made of wood, metal, or plastic—from a distance of 100 feet!

songs may be a way of binding the herd together. Or these huge sea mammals may actually share thoughts and experiences they have had during the year, much as human travelers in olden times shared tales around the fireside.

Based on the evidence known, few scientists would claim that humpbacks are exchanging com-plex messages. Yet, the ever-changing songs of the humpback remain a mystery.

Challenges for the Future

Whales other than humpbacks also fill the ocean with their amazing and beautiful sounds. The blue whale makes what is probably the loudest noise of any animal. These enormous creatures can make themselves heard above the background noise of the ocean for tens or even hundreds of miles. Yet that may not be very far compared to the distances whale calls may once have traveled.

Very large cetaceans, such as the blue whale and its close relative the fin whale, produce sounds that cover an extremely wide range. Some of these sounds are too low for human ears to hear, and others are too high. Today, because of the constant throb of ships' propellers, the ocean is a comparatively noisy place. But until 150 years ago, it was much quieter. Centuries ago, whales were able to hear each other's cries over a far greater distance. According to some scientists, the deepest moans of creatures such as the blue and the fin whale may have carried through seawater for thousands of miles. If this is true, then any two whales could have heard each other's calls, even if they were on opposite sides of the ocean.

There are many unsolved mysteries surrounding the whales. Perhaps, in years to come, scientists will be able to decode the whales' language so that we can understand what they are communicating to one another. Or we may find that cetaceans think in such a different way from humans that we shall never unlock the secrets of their songs.

In recent years, scientists have made much more progress in communicating with apes. But this has not been achieved by learning the details of how apes send messages to one another. The apes' own language seems to fall well short of what these creatures are actually capable of expressing. Instead, the real breakthrough in ape-human communication has come by teaching chimpanzees and gorillas to use a version of our own language.

At the Kewalo Basin Marine Mammal Laboratory at the University of Hawaii, Dr. Louis Herman is now carrying out similar experiments with dolphins. Herman and his staff have taught two dolphins, named Phoenix and Akeakamai, to respond to about 40 different whistle sounds. These sounds stand for words such as *fetch, ball,* and *frisbee.* The dolphins understand short sentences made from these words. What is more, they seem to understand the importance of the order of words in a sentence—an ability that not even apes possess. As research in this field advances, some exciting years may lie ahead in our efforts to share thoughts with other species of life on earth.

Hands On

Observe communication and behavior among social insects by keeping your own ant colony. A plastic home for a small ant colony can be bought ready-made, or you might try making the one of wood and glass shown here. Put soil in the nest chamber and transfer part of an ant colony to the food chamber. Since the ants are isolated from the outside, you will have to supply them with food such as honey, tiny pieces of raw meat, moist bread, and dead insects. Also, make sure that the soil in the nesting area is kept damp.

Observe how the workers build a new nest, with separate places for the eggs and larvae. What happens when you put in some fresh food? How do the workers communicate with one another? How does the ants' activity vary throughout the day and night? What happens if you introduce some new ants after the colony is established? Try other experiments, such as varying the light level in the feeding area or laying a scent trail across one of the notches to the nesting area. Keep a logbook of your observations.

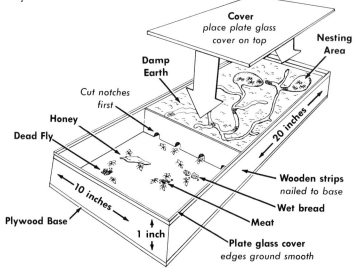

Cover
place plate glass cover on top

Nesting Area

Damp Earth

Cut notches first

Honey

Dead Fly

20 inches

Wooden strips
nailed to base

10 inches

Wet bread

Plywood Base

1 inch

Meat

Plate glass cover
edges ground smooth

Glossary

apes—apes belong to the same large group of animals as lemurs, monkeys, and human beings. Together, this group is known as the primates. Apes are large, tailless primates, more intelligent than monkeys, that swing through the branches of trees using just their arms

bivouac—a temporary camp built hastily using whatever materials are available. The "bivouac" made by army ants uses no material at all other than the living bodies of the worker ants hooked together by their legs

cetaceans—the scientific name given to the sea mammal group that includes whales, dolphins, and porpoises

communicate—to communicate is to send and receive information

cortex—in humans and more advanced mammals, the large outer part of the brain that handles abstract thinking. Our ability to talk, reason, plan ahead, and remember things from the past is centered in the cortex

echolocation—the process by which whales send out sound waves and interpret their reflected echoes to determine what objects lie around them

extinct—no longer living anywhere on earth; many animal and plant species have become extinct

gesture—a sign made by moving part of the body. For example, when we nod it is a gesture to show that we agree with something. Many animals use gestures to exchange messages

Hertz—a unit used to measure the frequency of sound. It gives the number of waves of sound that pass a certain point each second

instinct—something an animal can do without having to learn it. For example, it is an instinct for a baby to cry. Instincts are passed on from one generation to the next at birth. A great deal of animal behavior, especially among simpler creatures, is instinctive

language—a system used by an animal to communicate with others of its kind or with other species

Luna moth—a beautiful pale green moth, native to North America, that has a long slender tail and hind wings

macaque—a type of monkey with a long snout like that of a dog. There are several species of macaques living in Asia and Africa. Two of the Asian species, the Toque macaque and the Japanese macaque, are mentioned in this book

pitch—how low or high a sound is

posture—the positioning of the body in such a way that it has a certain meaning to others who are watching. For example, a dog will posture by pinning back its ears and drooping its tail when afraid

predator—an animal that hunts and eats other animals which are its prey. For example, a lion is a predator, and zebra are among its prey

social—a social animal is one that always lives in groups with others of its kind. Such creatures can defend themselves better against predators and find food more successfully than most other animals. Monkeys, prairie dogs, and termites are social animals

species—animals of a certain species have many important features in common. Most importantly, males and females of the same species can breed with one another to produce young

symbol—a written sign, such as a letter or a simple picture, that conveys information

territorial—a territorial animal is one that considers some area of land, air, or water to be its own and will defend it, especially against others of its kind. Sometimes a group of animals, such as a pack of hyenas, will "own" a territory

vervet monkey—a medium-sized, tree-dwelling monkey from Africa whose diet consists largely of fruit

vocabulary—the range of words or calls an animal can make that have a specific meaning. Human vocabularies consist of tens of thousands of words that can be put together in countless ways. Animal vocabularies are much smaller and less complex

Index